HEROES

Christy Ducker

with illustrations by
Emma Holliday

smith|doorstop

Published 2016 by
smith|doorstop books
The Poetry Business
Bank Street Arts
32-40 Bank Street
Sheffield S1 2DS

Text copyright © Christy Ducker 2016
Illustrations copyright © Emma Holliday 2016
All Rights of the Author and Illustrator Reserved

ISBN 978-1-910367-61-2
Typeset by Utter
Cover image: detail from Holliday Junction, by Emma Holliday
Printed by Biddles Books

Acknowledgements
With thanks to Arts Council England and Active Northumberland for their generous support. *Heroes* was also made possible by Victoria Coxon, Keith Gilroy, Keith Merrin, and the archivists at Woodhorn's Northumberland County Archive.

Thanks also to: Phyllis Christopher, Clive Gray, Emma Holliday, Jenny Larby, Claire Malcolm, New Writing North, and the Women Poets group in Newcastle.

smith|doorstop books are a member of Inpress: www.inpressbooks.co.uk. Distributed by Central Books Ltd., 99 Wallis Road, London E9 5LN

The Poetry Business gratefully acknowledges the support of Arts Council England.

Contents

for my family
– Christy

for Smart, Grace and Ruby, with thanks for your encouragement, inquisitiveness and support during the lino printing season
– Emma

Help for Heroes

Sometimes the bravest thing you can do
is learn how to look in the rearview
again, without panic, drive over
potholes without that fear, manoeuvre
through crowded markets and queues, or bedrooms
without a knife. You can't presume
it'll ever end, but might dismantle
this pain you're in, dreadnought grey panel
by panel, if you can just begin to talk
about Fallujah, Abu Ghraib, take
deep breaths and let out nightmares.
If you can talk about the pictures
that spool in your head (of stoning chickens
to cope, or swerving to hit a civilian
on purpose) then you'll have courage
as sharp as shears. Cut through the tonnage
of what's contained you, vent its hold,
strip out the guns, and tell the world
that what they saw on TV wasn't
war, but something much more distant –
you've brought the battle home with you,
and sometimes the bravest thing we can do
is hear you, stay you, and help you speak.

Meridian

What they didn't know was her brain
was a world that went on turning

even after they'd forced it down
the long grey chute of coma –

that when she woke, the hemispheres
would parley, how nations can

translate, on each other's behalf,
new circuits. Her bright message

lights up, *one child, one teacher,*
one book, one pen. Though she's altered

she tilts towards the sun, still
bickers with siblings, can't cook,

loves pink and *Bajrangi Bhaijaan.*
They didn't know she'd purge worms

from the education of girls –
her face opens out from its prime

meridian, sad to the east,
fierce to the west. She stands as straight

as noon and raises her medals,
her garland of A's, her hopes

to the sky with hands touching,
and I will set my clock by her.

South Shetland Islands

William Smith

At 55° North, he's wrong
as a map folded back on its own seams,
unreadable to the bankruptcy clerks
who write him as zero, then break his boat

but at 62° South, he was right
as the fact of land. Antarctica mapped
itself onto him and he opened out
as vistas, cinder, paths through penguin-stench

the way at 64° South he was right
to imagine continuous land
bucking eastward; its bays of whales, its fissures,
its total lack of concern claimed him

meaning, at 33° South he felt wrong,
in a sweat among mangoes and brown breasts,
when he'd poured himself into that bottle
he threw overboard much further South

along with the message of what he found,
a list of names he gave the islands,
none of which stuck, his common name gone
off the map, bobbing at landless latitudes.

After I Dazzle Napoleon,

I receive a letter from hell,
trusting me to find the answer
to miners who've been killed by coal
gas explosions and dark stuntings –
it's known that I ignite diamonds,
distill laughter through glass funnels,
and set loose the world's elements,
though I know the answer's restraint
this time, not my usual flash
but a version of light that's sieved
to its keenest behind thin mesh,
where it burns as cool as men's lives
constellating underground
with my safety lamp their godsend.

worth knowing

there was this girl
who grew to love dancing,
and lipstick and lacquer, and suits,
her difficult husband, her very own
five children (and didn't know that I couldn't
have children, or how she became the reason
I could, in the end, spark a child in a lab and bloom)
this girl had scraps of school and money, a knot in her womb,
and a whole white county of hospital doors that slammed,
apart from one that yawned and swallowed her name, even
her body's own cells (she didn't know doctors like mine who ask
for consent, who jacknife cancer with knowledge won
from peering into her) this girl is dead but also alive
in ways that disturb her children, because there is more
of her now than when she walked on earth, so many
million tonnes of her, stretching around the planet
in one continuous ribbon, her gift (together
with sugar dipped in vaccine, these big straight legs
she allowed me for free) this girl sells
for hundreds of dollars per batch online
though her family scrabble for health
and talk amongst themselves
about Henrietta
(HeLa)

The Archivists

They know it's serious
which is why they tie knots
so tight, and why they interlace

birth and death records in neat lots
on the flat calm of steel shelves.
Keepers of what you forgot,

they could reconstruct your whole life,
using just one fact, no bigger
than a gene. Here to solve

the puzzle of your future
by way of the past, they riddle
through vaults and tease structure

from what might seem junk. The bundled
information, history's DNA
dances at their fingers, shuttles

across the microfiche in displays
of what they'd love us to hold
dear. The archivists smile, in a way

that's wobbly, because they know
when books get burnt or regimes change,
they're always the first to go.

Josephine Butler's Psalm

The love of my life has gone
but I must live a life of love.

My daughter fell to her death
but I must mother fallen women –

I feed them second chances
but my critics chew on rage.

My critics churn the surface
but street-women sink like ships.

My critics try to burn me alive
but my life is already on fire.

When the world is raining stones,
what matter the bruise in my heart?

When I'm rising up to speak,
what matter the stones men throw?

Spice Girls vs. Aprilia

In a contracted room
the Law stares down as cool
as an icon, insisting
these women must stay young,
must move everywhere
on ten legs, that only
a dress as short as a vest
is a *true representation*.

But out on the road, one bolts
and refuses to be taken
as read – she re-writes a clause,
becomes the Spanish hermit,
extortionist, has-been, happy
adult scooting through mountains
at speed, where she catches up
on herself while the wheels turn.

Grace Darling's Dress

I was cut out for lounging in houses
but stitched into exile by Thomasin,
a woman happy to bastardise
my chances with two sets of hooks down my back –
the broad fit for her, the narrow for Grace.
There was no life, whoever I clung to
since Thomasin's face had burst from its seams
and Grace, the pretty one, courted extremes
alone at sea. She'd sweat me through
then spat me in blood each wild duck chase –
she shot like a man, with a hunter's knack
for effacement. I try to sympathise
now I'm restored – I put emphasis on
how flouncy I am, how tiny she was.

Wishing Well

Superheroes were never my thing –
I always preferred people, the ones
who have at least two sides, well-thumbed
as pennies, people who offer
ideas you can hold in your hands like a map,
a vaccine, a lamp, or a voting slip,
people who ask for *please-no-fuss*
when they bring a new bird into English
or stand at a lectern and sing,
people who wrestle with terror for life,
or swaddle the past in brown paper –
these heroes make me wish beyond
my own dark, how a well might wish,
something of them will fall through me like change.

Notes

Help for Heroes

'Mental trauma is taking an escalating toll on British servicemen and women' say Combat Stress, the veterans' mental health charity. In 2015 alone, there was a 19% increase in rates of PTSD amongst veterans. 1 in 10 of the UK's homeless population are ex-soldiers, many of whom are affected by PTSD.

Meridian

Malala Yousafzai (b. 1997) is a Pakistani-born education and equalities activist. She was shot by the Taliban in 2012, in an attempt to silence her advocacy of education for girls. She recovered and went on to campaign internationally for equal rights. In 2014, she won the Nobel Peace Prize, making her its youngest ever recipient.

William Smith

William Smith (b. 1790) was a Northumberland-born sea captain who traded coal around the world. In February 1819, he discovered Antarctica. The British authorities did not believe him. He sailed again in October 1819 to prove his point. In 1820, the Royal Navy sailed with him on a third voyage, to corroborate his claims. Soon after, William Smith was declared a bankrupt. His ship was broken up and he died a pauper in 1847.

After I dazzle Napoleon,

Humphry Davy (b. 1778) was a Cornish-born scientist and inventor. His many discoveries, and sheer charisma, led to success at an early age. To relax, he partook of nitrous oxide with Robert Southey and Samuel Taylor Coleridge. Napoleon awarded Davy a medal for science, even though Britain and France were at war. Davy saved thousands of lives by inventing the miner's safety lamp, which kept flame and coal-gas separate.

worth knowing

Henrietta Lacks (b. 1920) was an African-American woman whose cells were used to create the first immortal line for medical research. Lacks died of cervical cancer in 1951. Her cells were taken without her knowledge or her family's consent. 'HeLa cells' have been used to create the polio vaccine, to unlock the human genome, and to develop cancer treatments; they have been taken up Everest, and to the Moon. There are enough HeLa cells on earth to wrap around the Equator three times. HeLa cells can be bought online. Lacks's family never received any payment for their use. They cannot afford health insurance.

Josephine Butler's Psalm

Josephine Butler (b. 1828) was a Northumberland-born proto-feminist and social reformer. Intensely religious, she campaigned in particular for women's education and the rights of prostitutes. In 1863, Butler's six-year-old daughter, Eva, fell to her death in front of her. Butler said this trauma drove her to champion people in even more misery than herself. Her critics tried to stone her, and suffocate her by setting fire to the venues where she spoke.

Spice Girls vs. Aprilia

In 2000, the Italian scooter company, Aprilia took the pop band, Spice Girls to court for misrepresentation. The intention had been to launch a range of 'fashionable, fresh and cheeky' scooters, endorsed by the whole band. The orange model was to feature an image of Geri Halliwell, 'Ginger Spice'. However, Halliwell had grown frustrated by the restrictions placed upon her by celebrity. She left the band and breached the Aprilia contract.

Grace Darling's Dress

Grace Darling (b. 1815) was a Northumberland-born lighthouse keeper. In 1838, she helped to rescue nine people from a shipwreck. This deed coincided with mass-print and mass-marketing, so Darling became the first working-class celebrity. She preferred fishing, and shooting ducks to fame. She shared dresses with her sister, Thomasin. Many of these dresses had two sets of fastenings: Thomasin was curvy; Grace was tiny and slender.

About the author

Christy Ducker is a poet and tutor. Her first full-length collection, *Skipper* (2015) includes work commended by the Forward Prize judges. *Skipper* is described by Jackie Kay as 'deft and tough', and by D. Nurkse as 'important work by a powerful poet'. Christy's pamphlet, *Armour* (2011) was a PBS Pamphlet Choice.

Christy is currently Artist in Residence with York University's Centre for Immunology, and director of the North East Heroes writing project. Her PhD work at Newcastle University was awarded the 2015 Ella Ritchie Prize.

www.christyducker.co.uk

About the illustrator

Emma Holliday is a painter and colourist who can also be found delving into the world of printmaking. Drawing is the root of all Holliday's work and an illustrative response to words has been an interesting thread throughout her career. Holliday has worked collaboratively with many writers as well as painting within libraries, bookshops and universities. She finds the literary approach inspiring and the working relationship very creative.

Originally from the south of England, Holliday is now based in the North East. Mostly self-taught, Holliday's work is vibrant and expressive. She exhibits at various galleries, as well as at Open Studio events and via her website www.emmaholliday.co.uk